I AM

Discovering Who You Really Are

Nanice Ellis

ISBN Number: 978-1-4276-3765-9

I danced upon the cold dark sun,

searching for warmth among the stars –

floating endlessly through a myriad of

extraterrestrial sounds and atmospheres.

Knowing not where I belong or who I am.

If only I could see my reflection in the stars

and identify some long forgotten memory.

Who am I?

I have asked myself this question since the first thought I could think. I have asked myself this question since the beginning of time. Always, looking, seeking, searching for the answer - believing that when I found the answer I would know who I am.

What I now know to be true is that the searching, seeking, the absolute analysis and the very question itself kept me from knowing who I truly am. As I searched for a single answer, I missed what was right in front of me.

I missed every reflection of who I am.
And now I know.

I AM ALL

I AM AS I AM

It was my mind that stopped me from knowing who I am. The mind can never perceive of anything that it cannot locate and define in one way or another — it can only perceive within the construct of mind. Ironically, my mind was also the first to jump in and answer the question - "Who Am I? ". The answers weren't answers at all — they were just directions and never the destination. I now understand that the mind is just a bridge to the doorway of truth and when we mistake the bridge for the destination, we miss the open door.

To find myself, I ultimately let go of the very thing that led me to the doorway of self—discovering. I now know that I could never know who I am without first surrendering the searcher - the seeker - the mind. Only in a state of mindlessness could I cross through the doorway. It is the only way without exception.

When I finally asked the question "who am I?" and refused to allow my mind to answer this question, did the absolute truth of who I am reveal itself to me - completely.

I AM…

I am everything.
There is nothing that I am not.
I am all.
I am whole.
I am you.
I am the birds.
I am the sky.
I am the Universe in the palm of my hand.

I am the quiet thunder and
the loud silence in between the booms.

I am the final page in a good book
and the first page in a new life.

I am power and strength and the knowing
that there is nothing to prove.

I am softness and steel swirling in the creation
of new worlds and endless possibilities.

I AM GOD

I AM SOURCE

I AM ONENESS

I am both God and the imagination of God. I am the imagined of GOD. I am God having infinite dreams all at the same time and while in the dream – forgetting the dreamer and even forgetting it is a dream - no matter. I am both the dreamer and the dream. I am everything. I am nothing. I AM anything.

I AM PERFECTION

I am the dying and hopeless woman in a concentration camp. I am her dead husband. I am her tortured child. As much as I am the tortured, I am no less the torturer. I am innocence and betrayal. I am the stench of death and the sweetest smell of a blooming rose bud in the midst of desolation. I am Hitler and his army. I am hate. I am love. I am all. No matter how many lifetimes I have been denying this indisputable truth, it has existed all the while — without consciousness or consideration.

I am good and bad and discover myself to be innocent even in the most heinous of acts. When I embrace my innocence, I can no longer tell the difference between good or bad. Together they swirl in a smorgasbord of delight and horror - one not being any better or even preferable than the other. Only when I truly understand that, can I possibly KNOW I am all that is. - without exception.

> I am all the people I betrayed and hurt.
> I am loss and faith.
> I am creation and destruction.
> I am the knowing that one cannot
> exist without the other.
>
> I am the acceptance and
> judgment of all that is.
> I am all experience.
> I am things I have not yet discovered.

I am the greatest joy that explodes when I completely surrender to the bottomless depth of my sorrow and the realization that the battle of my resistance was the only thing that ever caused me pain.

I AM LIGHT

I am the powerful north wind making passionate love to fields of life-full sunflowers.

I am a devastating earthquake and the aftermath of crushed lives. I am all the opportunities of crisis that bring people together.

I am unfolding, unraveling -loosening.

Awakening.

I am intrinsically awake - even in the deepest of slumber.

Who I am is always conscious, whether I have known that before this day or even if I forget it upon awakening in the morning. I do not need to know who I am in order to go on creating and being all of who I am.

I am stillness and the movement that births itself from the womb of stillness.

I am the stillness that burns silently through every breath I breathe.

I am the no-matter of matter

I AM DARKNESS

I AM LUCIDITY

I finally know that I am the first breath
of every life – and the last.
Without favoring one or the other,
I am the fascination of both.

I am the cherisher of life – honoring life in every moment, yet never sacrificing life in exchange for the illusion of security - that would be no life at all. How frightened I must have been to ever "kill living" in exchange for an empty life – an infinitely immeasurable price to pay! Now I know.

I am the minuscule drop of water on the wings of a butterfly in flight for the first time. I am the dying cocoon left behind – recycled to dust that blows without hesitation or direction in the gentle wind.

I am infinity.

I AM GOD knowing itself in infinite beautiful ways, even when those ways appear to be ugly and distasteful to the human mind of limitation and rules. How cleaver that I am also the rules and limitations - and I am the rebelling against the rules and limitations.

There is nothing that I am not. Yet, I am NOT too.

I am the time found in timelessness and the timelessness found in every micro-second of time. I am the ticking of the clock – clockwise and counterclockwise. Imagine - I once believed that time only went one way. Amazing.

I AM ILLUMINATION

I AM LUMINOSITY

If it can be dreamed in the mind of GOD,
I am that too.

Now I search for anything that I might not be, but as soon as I find it I realize I am that too. I will spend eternity searching for that which I am not. I won't be disappointed because I will never find it. Ahh, sweet failure — yes, I am that too.

I am the love of you.
I am the lover.
I am the loved.
I am you.

Oh bright star in the sky, please tell me where I cannot find myself. Oh endless pain of a search that has no end — but also no beginning. Now I find myself to be both the ending and beginning — and everything in between.

I am the living duality of illusion
I am the reality beyond the illusion.
I am the stillness of reality and
the chaos of illusion.

I am years of grueling physical training moving towards one moment of victory. I am the determination that proudly announces itself in the most painful moments of defeat. I am the mind that always wins over the body and the body whose pleas for mercy go unnoticed. I am the realization that the only race to win is within myself. I am the first crossing the finish line and the instant knowing that the journey was the prize. I am the disability that told everyone I was dreaming and the accomplishment of overcoming that disability that told them they were right. I am the knowing that the commitment to any dream knows no failure.

I AM CONSCIOUSNESS

I AM AWARENESS

I am the wrongly accused who loses his life to pay for someone else's crime and the agonizing surrender that frees him to find purpose, even in imprisonment. I am also his long awaited release into a world he no longer recognizes or has need for.

I am all.

I am every word I speak
and every sentence I make up.
I am the silence between words
and the emptiness between breaths.

I am empty space that acts as a blank
canvas awaiting my painting upon it.

Oh, sweet oneness. Now I KNOW.
I am you. You are me. Together we
continue this beautiful endless dance both
as the dancer and the creator of the dance.

I am the taste of cold icy water on a hot July
day. I am the single bead of sweat that sneaks
out beyond the perfect fitting suit. I am the
desire of ripping off every shred of clothing
and jumping into the public fountain. I am my
mother, spouse or poor friend bailing me out
of jail - and never letting me live it down.

I am the vital substance in all.

I am the volume control for all the
mind chatter in the world.

I AM BOUNDLESS

I AM LIMITLESS

There is only one.
I am that oneness constantly

re-creating and re-discovering itself.

I am the observer.
I am the observed.
I am fascination and that which fascinates me.
There is no end to what I am.
No end indeed.

I am the snow glistened trees, welcoming my
decent as I float on my skis through endless
clouds of fluffy white powder. I am the blaze
that later that year, takes them to ashes —
and the silent regrets of carelessness.

I am both fear and love at the same time.
I am the speaker and the listener.
I am time and no time dancing together
in a spiral of amusement.
I am expectation and disappointment.
I am free and I am imprisoned.
I am the victim and the victimizer.

I am the judge who had it in for me — how could I
have judged him for judging me when I am him too?

Now I see - there was no need to resist -
anything. How can I truly resist who I am?

I AM EVER EXPANDING

I am the depression that took many lives and the security of even more. I am the fear that made people do terrible things they never imagined possible. I am homelessness and scarcity that had no end. I am the strength and courage that comes from overcoming the greatest of challenges and knowing myself to be so much more than I ever imagined.

I am pain and pleasure and when I embrace the wholeness of who I am - I can no longer tell the difference between them. When I fully surrender to each, all I can feel is deep abundant bliss.

> I am gratitude and ungratefulness
> flying together unbounded.

I am the brightest of lights and the darkest of darkness - at the same instant in time, without competition.

I am the river running through a small town and I am the pollution that the river carries with her. How can I shun the polluter when I am that too?

I am the band-aid that gives dignity and pride to the toddler just learning to walk, and I am his mom who gets to "kiss it to make it better". I am the belief that kisses really do heal.

I AM ECSTASY

I AM NOTHINGNESS

I am consciousness and the
consciousness of consciousness.

I AM IMAGINATOR

I am too many bills and not enough money in a time of great need. I am the mother of a five year old who realizes her daughter is better left raised by someone else. I am the aunt who desperately wants her own child but loses one baby after another to fate, the carelessness of others and poor medical conditions. I am her tremendous loss finally filled with a blue eyed-angel that takes all her pain away. I am the dedication she swore that child and the miracle baby sister that surprised everyone years later. I am the love that mother felt for both children equally for the rest of her life and the secret that remained with her almost to death. I am the unfettered love that remained constant even after the truth was revealed and sisters became cousins.

I am beauty and ugliness and the beauty that reveals itself out of ugliness when I take the time to really look deep enough to see.

Sweet Surrender...

I AM CREATOR

I AM ENDLESS

I am the feel of a lover's touch hidden in endless valleys and rolling hills. I am the union of desire and seduction melting into the madness of passion. I am the loss of innocence exploding into waves of ecstasy. I am invisible space between the two as they dissolve into each other – not knowing where one begins and the other one ends.

I am the courage to leave the love of my life – because I love myself more.

I am both the hider and the seeker.
I am the masked and the unmasked -
knowing no difference.
I am the mask itself.
Could I be any other way?
If so, I am that too.
Divine.

I am running naked on a cold autumn night
under the protection of the moon and the
impending threat of being seen.
I am naked and I am shielded - and every
aspect in between - with no preference for
one or the other. Now I know who I am.

I am instant gratification and
prolonged delirious pleasure.

I am the gluttonous and the starving.
I am the hedonist and the victim of poverty.

I am the obese and the self-destructive and
the disgust I once felt for both.
I had no idea I was so asleep.

I am the ever-changing
perfection of imperfection.

I AM BEGINNINGLESS

I AM IMMEASURABLE

There is nowhere I cannot look and find myself - completely. Perfectly.

Now I know how beautiful and magnificent I have been all along - even in all the lifetimes that I lived totally asleep and perceiving myself to be helpless and lost.

I have somehow found myself in the rubble of false beliefs that ran infinite lives up to this moment. Now I find myself in truth - realizing that I have been truth all along – but I kept it a secret from myself. I have always been truth even when I couldn't see it. In the midst of unfathomable lies, I remained truth. For now I know that truth cannot be taken away and will constantly remain itself, no matter how many masks are put upon it - or taken off. Finally, I let all my guards down and surrender to who I really am - surrendering to the truth of my being - in every form and formlessness. Now I see clearly that everything is created from truth - it is the eternal energy that all manifestation is built upon. Nothing else could withstand our tortuous delusions.

I AM INFINITY

I am the peace that intrinsically comes from the true surrender and acceptance of chaos. I am the chaos that is divinely inherent in peace.

I am peace and I am chaos.

I am both confusion and clarity and the absurd notion that one could possibly be better than the other. How can clarity even exist without my sister confusion?

I am the eyes and body of God. I am God.

I am the heavenly snow that brought a boy and his girlfriend to ski freely in the wilderness and the deadly avalanche that abruptly stole her life and his heart. I am the spring thawing itself out from a brutal winter and finding life after death.

How can I judge the harsh winter when I now know that I am that too?

I AM ETERNITY

I AM MORE THAN I HAVE YET IMAGINED

I am boundless, limitless infinity,
spinning passionately out of control.

I AM ABUNDANCE

I am the reflection of myself in someone else's eyes. Of course, I am all eyes too. I am the seer and seen. I am the seer seeing the seen and the unseen. Fascinating.

I am the bully who brought me to tears day after day when I was too young to understand who I am — who she was. Now I understand — without question or inquiry.

I am the forgiver of violence and ignorance.

I am forgiving and unforgiving - and the innocence that is inherent in the forgiver and the unforgiving. How could I be any other way?

I am the consciousness of the dreamer.

I am the shadow in the cave —
believing itself to be real.
I am the prisoner in the cave mesmerized
by the distant hope of light

I am the sly forbidden look between lovers and the sweet feel between life-long friends.

I AM OVERFLOWING

I am overwhelming boundless joy and unstoppable tears, as I revel at my reflection everywhere I look.

I AM SATURATED IN PURE BLISS

I am cancer and the relentless battle of a teenage girl, trying to squeeze every moment out of life before her ultimate surrender. I am the hat she wore when all her hair fell out. I am the pain that not even morphine could overcome. I am the first kiss she never had and the beautiful dress she wore just months before death took her to another kind of prom. I am the deep gratitude for all the years she had the courage and strength to hang on, despite a progressively debilitated body that continuously failed her dreams and desires. I am the call I expected that told me she was gone and the tears I shared with those who loved her and wanted just one more moment. I am her final surrender and release out of a body that could no longer hold her mighty spirit. I am everything she was and everything she never grew up to be.

Oh great nothingness – I pray
to you for everything (I am).

Without hesitation, I am unconditionally granted all
that I both consciously and unconsciously pray for.
I pray to have the courage to look deep
enough beneath myself and beyond myself to
discover that no prayer goes unanswered.

I am the perpetual unfolding of
discovery. How perfect that I am both
the discoverer and the discovered.

I am the compilation of all those things that
are left unsaid and cleverly hidden behind
the fear of rejection and the revelation
of truth that always sets me free.

I am the heavy air awaiting precise instructions
from some greater force and the genuine
immediate release from this emotional prison.

I am the screen of projection and all I project.
I am the power to change the projector.

I am the wild current of rivers
running through infinite lives.

I AM WHOLE

I AM COMPLETE

I am the child playfully rolling down a hill and the mother who stops her with fear and impatience. Ahh yes! I am the mother and her mother's mother. I am the child I am yet to birth and even the one sent away before she could breathe her first breath of life. I am the giver of life and I am the taker away of life. Yes, now I see there is nothing that I am not. Nothing that I cannot be.

I AM LETTING GO

I am never ending perfection that I cannot stop creating - even when I forget to remember that it truly is perfection, or that I am the creator.

I AM THE ONE MIND

Now I see who I really am.
Can you see who you are?

Imagine just for a moment, that
you can — and then You Can.

Imagination is the link that draws non-matter
to life and the unavoidable gut-wrenching pain
that wraps itself around fears that have been
created through that which we imagine.

I am shock and infinite knowing.

I am man even as I am woman.

I am opening as I penetrate.
I am deep pounding penetration, piercing
through the dense physical form and
finding myself in spiritual realms of
power, certainty and playful wonder.

I am the impatience I discover as I'm standing in line
and the transformation to love as I recognize I am
still just one of a kind.

I am eternal patience and momentarily
impatience and I delight in both - equally.

I AM THE OBSERVER

I am the youngman who stared at the closed door, so long he missed the one that opened.

I AM STILLNESS

How divinely silly of me to be jealous of anything when I am that too? Is one breath jealous of the next? Or does it fulfill it's destiny and let go of all it was in order to become even more. Somehow it knows there is always even more – even in delicious excruciating bliss, there is always more. Yet I remember now to give myself fully to all and never hold back in anticipation that more is coming. How could it come when I withhold myself from the divine experience of this moment – even when my body and mind perceive agonizing pain, or the potential for abundant overflowing joy?

I am perpetual unfolding without conditions, expectations, or a huge payoff of some kind – which would cost me more than I ever care to give away. Yet, any cost is no cost at all when I am all that is.

I am the vicious animal attacking anything in it's path. I am also the attacked, screaming out for help that will not come. Have I been attacking myself all along?

> Now I see.
> I see the perfection of who I am
> and who I have always been.

I now understand that no matter how bad I failed – there is no failure. Impossible. So, how is it I am also failure? Interesting.

No matter what I do, I just can't make a mistake - even before I remembered who I really am. I am power and weakness and even in my weakest of states, how is it that I am still all powerful? How curious this all is.

> I am the conviction that all my beliefs
> are true and the truth that all beliefs
> are the illusion of my conviction.

I AM PURE ENERGY

I AM ELECTRICITY

I am a house of mirrors and the
silliness that I cannot find myself.

I am the smell of lilacs on the side of the road on the first day of school. I am small feet running twice as fast just to keep up with my father's normal stride. I am the feel of a tiny hand inside the rough but kind cocoon of his bigger one. I am my father's hopes spinning into my dreams and the eventual realization of both in the life of a grown woman. I am the legacy left behind – and the gratitude eternally felt for his unconditional support that extends beyond life.

I AM THE UNIVERSE

I AM AWARENESS

I am the rain and the drought - without competition or battle. And I am that too.

I am the frightened toddler who relentlessly clings to her mother to help her hide from the huge alien-like monster who lives in her closest.
I am the monster in her closest.
I am the mother of that frightened toddler embracing her magical powers with vigilance and absolute certainty that magic exists.
I am the realization that magic creates monsters — and destroys them.

I am all the magnificent colors that I see and even those I am yet to imagine into creation.

I am the philanthropist and the thief.
I am what has been stolen. I am all that is found.
I wonder how could I have stolen
from myself — when I am all?

I am the illusion of scarcity masked
as dollars and cents.
I am the reality of abundance
which knows no limitation

Now I understand what I failed to notice. How glorious — it is never too late to notice — and then everything changes, even the things that seemed done and past. There is no moment in eternity that is not affected when you wake up and NOTICE. Imagine every time you pay attention — when you notice ANYTHING without a story attached to it, you are directly affecting the grandchildren of your grandchildren's grandchildren. You are also instantly and directly affecting the father of your father's father and every father before him. Who would have thought?

I AM WHOLE

I AM THE CONSCIOUSNESS OF CONSCIOUSNESS

I am the all in everything and
everything in the All.

I am the sick man in Florence, Italy who just needed to be seen in order to heal. I am his grateful wife who gifted a slip of paper that unknowingly led to a miracle that called to be experienced.

I am the wind and the rain, the rocks and the sand.

I am endless space.

I am gravity and weightlessness.

I am every star in the sky — even when they fall from grace and burn up in the atmosphere — leaving only virgin fairy dust that can heal the most broken of hearts, deepest of sorrow and falsity of illusions. Do they understand that they are indestructible even when they appear to be lost or broken?

I am every planet known to exist and every planet yet to be discovered.

I am all of creation that has not yet been created. Imagine that.

I am tears and laughter.

I am shame and guilt.

I AM AS "IT" IS

I AM FLAWLESS

I am your soul, fighting against the dark in order to be the light – not yet knowing that only in the acceptance of both unconditionally can it free itself to discover who it has always been.

I am the final "I do" after a decade of not knowing. I am the courage and strength to love full heartedly and know when it's time to make a life-long promise. I am the single white lily in my soon-to-be daughter -in-law's bouquet and the adoring look on my son's face as she walks down the aisle. I am their union, their commitment and the love they took the time to create. I am the surprise that in that time I have also learned to love. I am the tears that roll down my face when I realize my son is marrying my daughter.

I AM SEEMLESS

I AM DANCING ENERGY

I am the healed, the healer - the healing.

I am both the red light and the green light and the absurd traffic accident that happened below, when the red and green forgot who they were.

> I am the construction worker that I blamed for making me late. How ironic that I am also lateness. And in my lateness, I am exceptionally early. How could I be otherwise?

> I am every note of every song.
> I am the unnoticeable silence
> between the notes.

I am the abandoned and the one who did the abandoning. How amazing that it was me who abandoned me all along? To think that I once blamed another. If only I knew. I do now.

Yes, I am wisdom and stupidity and I am the lover of both — needing one to have the other.

> I am the point of pointlessness and the meaning of meaninglessness.

> I am absolute pleasure unfolding
> into more delirious pleasure.

I AM SOUND OF CREATION

I AM THE ECHO OF BLISS

I am the hallucination of everything that I am. I am the hallucinator. And without that, nothing could exist. Unless of course it does.

I am the knowing of who you really are.

I am the magical dance of the sun setting over Athens in unforgettable splendor and carefree knowing that she can set a million times over and yet never tire of her own magnificence.

I am a new sun wiping away the darkness of a long night. I am fun in the sun and I am the sun having fun — delicious!

I am the words of flattery and the energy of criticism, knowing that at their core they are one in the same.

I am the pure openhearted experience of acceptance.

I am pride, prejudice and the beautiful game played by both — Bravo!

I am a Nothing unfolding into everything and everything collapsing into Nothing.

I AM TIMELESS

I am the seal balancing on a giant red ball in the circus — finding it's balance as it loses it at the same time. Now I am confused. Was it the seal or the ball that was seeking balance? Oh yes., now I see it is the seal and the ball both striving towards the unpredictable experience of balance. I am the knowing that balance can only be mastered when you have given yourself plenty of time and space to experience collapse and crisis — and then find the middle in between.

> I am unbalance seeking balance
> and balance seeking to let go.

I AM I AM NOWHERE

When I compare myself to anything,
I fool myself to believe that I can be
any better or worse than anything
else. How could I be, when I am also
that which I compare myself to - how
beautifully absurd. Now I know.

I am unfolding perpetual discovery. How amazing that I am both the discoverer and the discovery.

Now I see, there is no place to hide
from who I really am.
I find myself in every secret hiding place.

I am every place and the placelessness
in which the place exists.

I am the laughter and tears of three great
women who journey together throughout
the world and within their hearts — knowing
one journey cannot be embarked without the
other. I am the moment I knew that I would
not take the journey of my life alone.

I am the open door that beckons
you to walk through it.

I am the sweetness of my teenage son's first kiss.

I am perfection unfolding into even more perfection.

I am perfection honoring my perfection as
it transforms itself and me into even higher
vibrations.

I AM EVERYWHERE

I AM AGELESS

I am.
I just am.
I am just as I am.

I am the shininess of a frozen lake and the feel of sharp blades, pressing unmercifully upon me — chipping away. I am the frigid rain storm that unexpectedly rolls in the very next day and fills in the gaps where the ice showed increasing signs of losing her stability. I am five-years-old and afraid that if I step foot on the ice, it will crack and, without warning, I will be violently sucked under the dense prison of frozen water - and in quiet helpless desperation I will let go of my life. I am the imagined pain and regret that my parents will undeniably experience when they realize that they made me go on the ice despite my pleas for escape. I am the memory of imagination and the gratitude that most fears go un-manifested.

I AM THE EMBODIMENT FOR ILLUSION — SEEMING REAL.

I AM INDEFINABLE

I am the very last beat of a frightened heart as it passes to another vibration where hearts are painted on canvas and displayed proudly with pride and courage.

I am the heart that the loss of one life
provided for the life of another.
I am the cellular memory that will
always exist in that heart.

I am a family's last chance before the finalization of a divorce that will ultimately break down the family union. I am the knowing that breakdowns are most often the cause of break ups.

I am the power and promise of eroticism that whispers in our ears and shouts from down below.

I am the projection of God
in anyway I choose.

I am the surprise of a fresh spring day in the middle of a long winter – and the promise of more to come.

I am the river that floats me downstream
to my favorite place in the Universe.

I AM UN-RESTRAINABLE

I am the new grandmother who sat in the coffee shop passionately composing a poem for a brand new grandson. I am the already grown grandson who finds the poem in the back of an old dresser and feels the intense love of his grandmother, even though it has been many years since her passing. I am his newborn son who will know his great grandmother through words written a life time ago - in the middle of a coffee shop.

I AM LAWLESS

I am the rhythmatic heart beat of first
   love, blossoming to the surface.

I am wonderment and complete
knowing, dancing together to celestial
music they just co-created.

I am the broken stiletto on my right foot.
I am the foot,.
         the shoe,
                  divinely broken.

I am the letting go of everything I believed to be
   true as I am the discoverer of eternal truth.

I am the soft lips of a woman hanging
blissfully onto the hardness of a man.

I am as much words without judgment as I am
the judgment of the words.

Ahh, blissful surrender to the knowing of who I really
am. How could it have taken me so long to awaken
and yet no time at all?

         I am pure potential.

I am my German Sheppard who bled to death on my six-year-olds lap on the way to the animal hospital. I am the tears I shed as I embraced the reality of death. I am the wisdom of my eight-year-old son, who clearly told me that death is an illusion and there is nothing to cry about. I am the stench of death that strongly lingered in my car for many months. I am the car I sold to rid myself of death's reminder.

I AM INCLUDED WITHOUT CONSIDERATION

I am obsessive compulsive
and absolute letting go.

I am the precise synchronicity of the Universe.

I am the Universe.

I am the depths of depression and the endless heights of ecstasy.

I am dense water expressing itself as a glimmering, frozen hillside. I am the hidden hot spring located on that hillside joyously bubbling up from the center of the earth.

I am the suddenly humbled king of the land,
kneeling down to see himself – for the first time .
I am the innocence of a child's smile etching into his
memory for eternity.
I am the milk left by the door
in the middle of the night.
I am the starving mother who stole it
to feed her baby.
I am the understanding and forgiving that reminds
me to look beyond the act and see the innocence.

I am the bottomlessness of the infinite void and the shallowness of thinking the void is something to avoid.

I AM MINDLESS

I AM ACCEPTANCE

I am the first cry of a baby girl as the doctor lifts her from her mothers open stomach. I am the father who holds back tears of relief and the mother who wails with joy. I am the instant melting away of all the years of failed pregnancies and deceased hopes. I am the unfolding of faith in miracles and the absolute possibility of impossibility.

I am the point of no return and the relief that the choice is over.

I am the last bud of creation sitting hopefully on a nearly dead tree branch - and the possibility of life springing forth.

I am the first bud of a new earth.

I am the fear that stops you from knowing who you really are and the love that will ultimately reveal itself in you.

I am the question as much as I am the answer and the knowing that one cannot exist without the other.

I am every boarded up window and locked door.

I am all the energy I used to stop living my life for too many years to count.

I am the realization that there is NOTHING to complain about.

I AM EMPTINESS

I AM VIBRATION

I am the no-thinking that happens when
I let my heart lead and my mind follow.

I am the single strand of gray hair protruding loudly from my grandmother's chin.

I am the sharp blade that removes the hair that society says shouldn't be growing where it is.

I am the acceptance and judgment of both.

> I am you before you have remembered who you really are and the knowing with even the slightest bit of doubt you are still in the process of remembering.

> I am the moment of overwhelming awakening that awaits you.

> I am the love that exists in everyone and everything, regardless of circumstance.

I am the unseen part of the crescent moon and the wonderment of what else has not yet revealed itself.

I am deep and abundant, sobbing over beauty hidden all around me — because I am all that too. If only I knew.

> I am the beholder of the "DREAM"

I AM WAVES OF POSSIBILITIES

I AM BEING

I am the impossibility of making a mistake
and the illusion of punishment or karma.

I am all the times I ever held back because of fear of
losing myself or getting hurt.
And now I wonder....
To what could I have lost myself?
To what could I have been hurt?
When I am all that is.
Yes, now I know.

I am the blind and in my blindness I can clearly see.

I am my filters and false beliefs that have
kept me from seeing all there is to see.

I am the infinite space between the
in-breath and out-breath.
Oh how I have wondered what
happens in that space.
Yes, now I know — everything
and nothing at all.

I am the medium who shares the gift of communicating
with beings and non-beings and the realization that
there is no difference between being and not being.

I am the melting of me into you and
the melting of us into ALL.

I AM POWER

I AM INDESTRUCTIBLE

I am both sides of every war. I am everyone who has killed in the name of religion, ownership, or to prove something. I am the bullet that kills the eighteen-year-old son and his devastated and lost mother. I am the flag that lies over his coffin justifying his senseless death. I am knowing that even in the defeat or victory of war - nothing is ever lost or gained and that life cannot be created or destroyed.

I AM EVER FLOWING

I am the knower of the unknown.

How did I forget to remember - I am also the Earth?

How perfect that I am also the remembering.

I am the old worn leather chair waiting for its ride to the dump. I am the helpless lamb whose life was intrusively and violently stripped away for the carelessness of temporary comfort. I am the intrinsic wisdom of the lamb who will one day know who it is.

I am as much loving without conditions as I am hatred as far as the mind can travel.

I am the self loathing that comes from decades of abuse and intimate betrayal and I am the freedom and discovery of who I really am.

I am fear and insecurity masking itself as love, and the love hidden beneath both.

I am the surprise of a fresh spring day in the middle of a long winter – and the promise of more to come.

I am the web of imagination and the imagination that creates the web.

I AM THE ONE

I am the limitless experiencing limitation.

I AM IMAGINATION

I AM THE SEER

I am all the money in the world pretending to have power over us.

I am all the money in the world frightened to death because it knows we will one day find out it's dirty little secret and it's illusion of power will be lost forever.

I am desperate confusion and fear as my dad clung to life as death pulled him away. I am the painful sound of the respirator that worked 24 hours a day for two months to prolong his ultimate death. I am every cigarette he ever smoked and I am the judge and jury of his life-long flirtation with suicide. I am the misguided love of my mother who insisted that he live at any cost. I am my father's loyalty to my mother, which made him hang on until she was ready to let him go. I am his spirit following me around and looking over me.

I AM THE OBSERVER

I AM MAGNIFICENT

I am the despair that comes with loneliness and I am the tranquility that aloneness makes available. I am the distinction between the two.

> I am the awaiting of what I have
> already found – or has it found me?

> I am every man who has ever bruised
> my body or broken my heart. I am the
> effortless forgiveness that comes from
> recognizing we are all innocent.

I am the mature flower giving freely of her nectar and the bumble bee who hasn't yet discovered it shouldn't be able to fly.

> I am the remembering of who I
> am – and have always been.

> I am the illusion of separation and
> the oneness of the dreamer.

I am the sound of hooves on the roof in the minds of sleepless children. I am the hands of the clock that refuse to move and the teasing sun that begins to rise before the night is done. I am the robust scent of coffee as it drifts up the stairs announcing the end of a long wait and the final ripping of paper and bows in the rush to reveal. I am the memory of overwhelming anticipation that still lingers after all these years.

I AM DELIGHT

I AM PASSION

I am a blazing candle melting
itself into infinity.

I am all the spiritual bypasses that happen when someone wants to believe that he is more evolved than he really is — all the while missing the valuable lessons that could have gotten him there by now.

I am an unspoken whisper echoing through eternity, effortlessly composing the sounds of the Universe. Bliss.

I am the conversation that opens new doors to the personal journey that begins to unfold.

I am perfection revealing itself once again. Does it ever end? Why should it? Unfathomable.

I am one energy working in harmony with itself.

I am electricity lighting the world.

I am the smile on my face when I see who you really are.

I AM DESIRE

I AM MOVEMENT

I am awakening from an amazing hallucination
and discovering who I really am.

I am spellbound – in infinite possibilities.

I am the giggling of silliness and the
discomfort of asking for help.

I am the in-breath and the
out-breath of Bliss, refreshing itself

I am the play called "Life"
I am the script writer who makes it up
as he goes along.
I am the producer who puts all the
details in order.
I am the builder of the stage who creates the
perfect setting for a show to go on.
I am the actor who is discovering himself to
be more than an "actor".
I am the director who reminds all involved to
release fear and expectations and just enjoy
the show.
I am the audience sitting on the
edge of their seats wondering how
it will all turn out – perfectly.

I AM WORDLESSNESS

I know who I am.
I know who I am - I have always been -
beyond time and space.
I am now who I always will be.

When I know who I am, I also know who you are. You are everything that I am. You are everything and nothing. You are perfect in all your seeming imperfections. You are a gift from GOD and all the while you are the giver and receiver. You are love and beauty. You are infinity swirling around inside your body — cradling you to bliss. You are bliss.

As you remember that you *are* everyone and everything, you awaken to the revelation that you are part of the ONE as much as *you are the ONE.* When you finally know that there is no other, you stop searching for the magic answer that will set you free. You are free. You always have been. There is nothing that you can imagine and manifest that will ever hurt you. Go ahead and try. Impossible.

Whether you now know yourself to be GOD or are yet to awaken to this knowing — you are GOD. You are GOD without conditions or limitations. There is nothing that you can do in your wildest imagination that will ever stop GOD from being GOD. It is who you are. I know this because it is who I am and if I am also you, there can be no denying that you too are GOD.

I AM ISNESS

I AM BLISS

I am the deep refreshing breath of life you take in, and the sigh of relief that there was never anything to fear.

Have faith you are loved and even as you forget, you are remembering. It's all waiting for you but take your time - there is no rush. It's all perfection unfolding into more boundless perfection — Yes, you are that too. Now you know.

I am the last sleepless night
before awakening

I AM _____

_____

_____

_____

_____

_____

_____

_____

_____

_____

_____

I AM _____

_____

_____

_____

_____

_____

_____

_____

_____

_____

_____

I AM _____

_____

_____

_____

_____

_____

_____

_____

_____

_____

_____

I AM _____

_____

_____

_____

_____

_____

_____

_____

_____

_____

I AM

Radio Talk Show Host of "Chai with Nanice", Life Guru, Spiritual Guide, Speaker and Author of

- The Infinite Power of You!
- Even Gandhi Got Hungry and Buddha Got Mad!
- LipPrints
- What if...
- The Gratitude Journal

Nanice is available for Workshops, Presentations and Keynotes, as well as Tele-conferencing and One-on-One Coaching sessions.

Visit www.Nanice.com for current radio show times, podcasts, insightful articles, life enhancement quizzes, free downloads and to order more books!

WWW.NANICE.COM
801.953.6490
Info@Nanice.com

Nanice Ellis

Discover Yourself